RECCE TECH

Osprey Colour Series

RECCE TECH

THE PHANTOM AND THE DRAGON LADY

PAUL F CRICKMORE

For my son, Matthew Alexander, and the late Bill Skliar

Published in 1989 by Osprey Publishing
Limited
59 Grosvenor Street, London W1X 9DA

© Paul F Crickmore 1989

British Library Cataloguing in Publication
Data
Crickmore, Paul F.
    Recce tech: Phantom and the Dragon Lady
    1. United States. Reconnaissance
    aeroplanes
    I. Title
    623.74'67'0973
ISBN 0 85045 908 7

Editor Dennis Baldry
Designed by Paul Kime
Printed in Hong Kong

Front cover Heat'n'Dust: gear up
(it has a limit speed of 250 knots),
flaps up and burner engaged, Lt Col
Chuck Chinnock (Commander of
the 192nd TRS) winds up the
altimeter

Back cover TR-1, 80-1074 gets
airborne from Beale on a night
training sortie

Title pages Watch the birdie: Lt
Col Chuck Chinnock and Brigadier
General Stephen Korcheck head out.
The forward looking oblique camera
is either a KS-72 or KS-87.
Manufactured by CAI, it can be
fitted with either a 3 or 6 inch focal
length lens

Opposite The author in an RF-4C
Phantom II of the 192nd TRS at
Reno

It is significant that the first military application of the aeroplane was as an observation platform. Through surveillance and reconnaissance, tactical and strategic intelligence reports are compiled, the rapid collection and dissemination of which is of fundamental importance in supporting the political and military decision-making process. The successful execution of a tactical or strategic reconnaissance mission, including the subsequent evaluation and interpretation of the information acquired, can be crucial. It is therefore imperative that personnel, platforms and sensors measure up to the demanding reconnaissance technical, or recce tech, task.

This book is a tribute to the men and women involved in the recce tech business and spotlights the two legendary platforms, namely the McDonnell Douglas RF-4C Phantom II—often referred to as the 'Rhino', and the Lockheed U-2/ER-2/TR-1, affectionately known as the 'Dragon Lady', because of its similarity to a dragonfly.

This colour series book would not have been possible without the help and co-operation of Cols Graham and Saboski, Lt Cols Chuck Chinnock and Bill Shepard, Majors Suzanne Randle, Joe Saxon, John Bowen and Brian Shul, Capt Bob Lylef, T/Sgt Ralph Langley, S/Sgt Kelly Godbey, Mr John Aveson, Jim Hoyt, Vern Eliason, Cathy Lowne, Dennis Baldry, Kev Gothard, Jane Harvey of Canon (UK) Limited, my dear friends Don and Anita Jensen and my wife Stephanie.

All photographs in this book, with the exception of four by Major John Bowen and annotated as such, were taken by the author at Beale AFB, Reno International Airport, Moffett Field and RAF Alconbury, England between August and October 1988. Canon camera equipment was used throughout loaded with Kodachrome 64 or 200 film.

Right Sitting on the ramp at Reno–Cannon International Airport, the crew of a 192nd TRS RF-4C Phantom II perform the final shutdown procedures on the aircraft before climbing out. This RF-4C wears the 'Egyptian One' scheme now becoming standard on all reconnaissance Phantoms

Contents

Low Level High Rollers 8

Rhino Recce 26

NASA 64

Dragons at Beale 72

Toujours au Danger 108

Low Level
High Rollers

Conceived following the National Security Act of 1947, the 192nd Fighter
Sqn of the Nevada Air National Guard was formed in 1948 at Stead Field,
Nevada, flying F-51 Mustangs. During its 40-year history the unit has also
flown the F-86, RB-57 and RF-101; collecting along the way several top
awards for professional excellence.

Funded in part by its home state and also by Federal dollars allocated by
the National Guard Bureau, the 192nd Tactical Reconnaissance Sqn (TRS) is
integrated into the US Air Force structure through the 152nd Tactical
Reconnaissance Group (TRG) which, if mobilized, would report to Tactical
Air Command.

Today this combat-ready asset flies the McDonnell Douglas RF-4C
Phantom II from Reno–Cannon International Airport, Reno, Nevada, where
they specialize in low level recce

Known as the High Rollers, the 192nd TRS launched sorties 9, 10 and 11
of Tuesday, 9 August 1988 at 18.30 hours, local time

Above Aircraft serial 029, call sign ARROW 33, formates on ARROW 31—lead. A European One camouflaged bird, serial 876, call sign ARROW 32, was the photo platform

Right Tracking 065 degrees and maintaining 21,000 feet en route to the Air Refuelling Contact Point (ARCP), the formation slips into close trail

High over the arid desert of northern Nevada, Colonel Bill Shepard, an ex-F-102 and One-O-Wonder pilot, cross controls 876 for a better shot of the other two aircraft

Air refuelling was conducted at flight level (FL) 220 in Area 648. Note the momentary fuel spray-back on boom disconnect

Left Flying into sun while on the boom or in close formation can be tricky. The tinted helmet visor becomes an invaluable asset

Above ARROW 31 (on the boom) was flown by Capt Tom Currence and his Guy In Back (GIB) was Flight Surgeon Colonel Charlie Filippini. ARROW 32 was crewed by ex-US Navy A-4 pilot Lt Col Jack Thomas and Capt Ted Zwicker, an ex-B-52 navigator, was his Weapons Systems Officer (WSO)

Left Our turn next: the KC-135 tanker, call sign UTAH 52, had come from Salt Lake City, and was part of the 151st Air Refueling Group

Above Once on the boom, the KC-135's co-pilot activates the fuel transfer pumps which send over 5000 pounds of JP-4 fuel into our tanks

Above Transit to the low-level route was conducted at medium altitude

Opposite above On reaching the low-level route the altimeters came down as the airspeed indicators climed

Opposite below At 30 feet and 500 knots the foreground was a blur— who said the Air National Guard can't fly low-level!

Jack Thomas eases 029's nose up for minimal ridge clearance. The F-4 is a superbly stable low-level platform, whose shape, size, weight, power and presence have given rise to this classic aeroplane's apt nickname—Rhino

Main picture Against a fast-setting sun and a recession of ridges, we complete the low-level sector of our route and pull up to medium altitude

Inset Tom Currence pitches 875 out of formation and heads for the Reno traffic pattern

Rhino Recce

Right Part of the ramp at Reno

Below Operational planning plays a key role in all aviation activity. To boost squadron funds during these times of tight budgetary constraints, the 192nd has diversified considerably and can offer several innovative and competitively priced services

Above Reconnaissance Air Meet (RAM) is a week-long biennial competition designed to enhance the skills of all involved in the tactical reconnaissance mission. Here a crew member puts the finishing touches to the nav plan that will take five aircraft down to Texas and RAM. Note unofficial shoulder patch

Right Out on the ramp a Montana ANG C-130 is loaded with equipment for the meet

Above Winners in 1986, the 192nd TRS came in a close second during the 1988 competition

Right Prior to the competition which is held at Bergstrom AFB, five 192nd aircraft deployed to Carswell AFB, also in Texas, to work up for one week. Major Nick Gullihur and Capt John Mason WSO, taxi 068, call sign ROLLER 31, off the ramp and pass local TV news teams from NBC and CBS

Left Last to leave were Capt Vandam and Major Wilkerson in 016, call sign ROLLER 35. All five aircraft were configured with two 370 gallon wing tanks, a 600 gallon centre tank and a slipper tank at station two (inboard the left wing tank) for carrying personal gear for the temporary duty (TDY) deployment

Above Of the five aircraft sent to Carswell only two, and forty personnel, will be permitted to represent the squadron in the competition

Above ROLLERs 33 and 34, crewed by Col Molini (CO 152nd TRG), Major Milne 1st Lt Turney and Major Hilsabeck depart to join the formation. After rendezvousing with COPPER 06, a KC-135 tanker, and taking on 50,000 pounds of gas, they proceed, low-level, to Carswell

Right Back at Reno: exterior inspection complete, a further 60 cockpit checks are made before cranking the engines

Taxiing: nose gear steering—engage and check. Wheel brakes—test. Pilot and WSO flight instruments—check operation. Pilot and WSO oxygen diluter lever—as required

Ground crews conduct a last-chance
check at the holding point to
runway 16 Right

Left Before take-off another 20 cockpit checks are made

Above Cleared by ATC to line-up and take-off, 870 moves towards the active

Main picture Half flap is recommended for all take-offs. The pilot applies the brakes and sets the throttles at 85 per cent with normal RPM response. Exhaust Gas Temperature (EGT) reads 450 degrees, just as it should, and fuel consumption running at 4000 pounds per hour. Quarter nozzle aperture is selected, oil pressure is at 30 to 40 psi and all cockpit warning lights are checked. Finally the nose gear steering is engaged, the brakes released and the throttles opened. 'Listen to that. No wonder rhino power makes me horny.'—F-4 pilot

Inset Oozing power from every pore: at 70 knots directional control passes to the rudder. Nose gear steering is disengaged. Prior to nosewheel lift-off speed, apply aft stick. As nose rises, control pitch attitude to maintain 10 to 12 degrees on the Attitude Director Indicator (ADI). At 52,000 pounds weight, fly-off is at about 180 knots

Tanking from a KC-135 is conducted at 315 knots indicated airspeed

Above Characterized by its remodelled nose section, the RF-4C has two side windows at station two, to enable KS-87 frame cameras, manufactured by CAI and fitted with a 3 or 6 inch lens, to shoot low-level oblique shots of targets left or right of the aircraft's track

Right Fast and low is the tactical recce pilot's key to battlefield survival

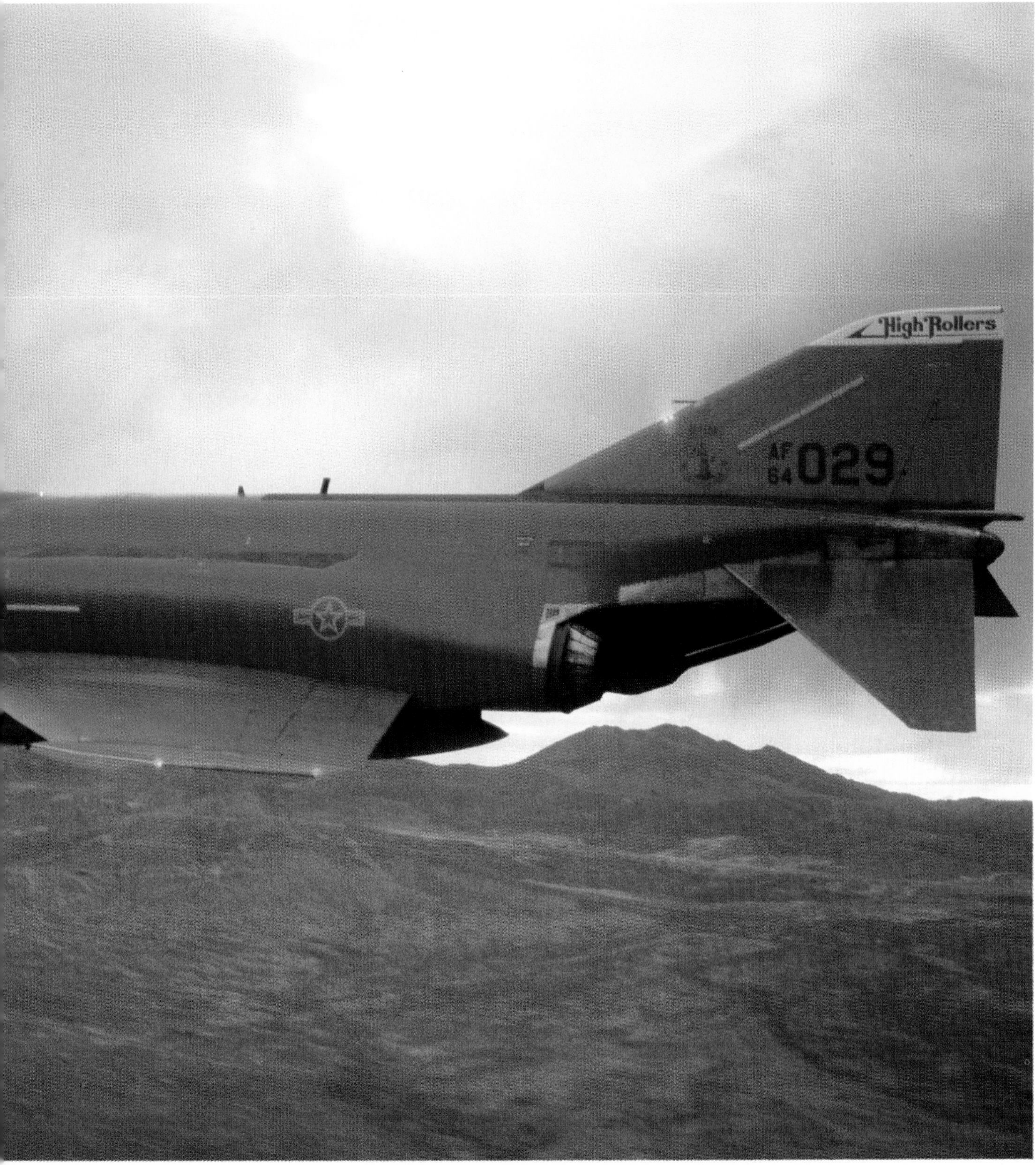
High Rollers
AF
64
029

Above On speed, the angle of attack indicator displaying between 18.7 and 19.6 units, 017 comes home for an oiler landing. Jettisoning a 16-foot ringslot type drag chute stowed in the empannage significantly reduces landing roll distances

Opposite above Brake chute door still agape, this green bird taxies in to roost

Opposite below Despite their age, ANG aircraft are maintained in immaculate condition

Opposite above A vertically mounted Fairchild KA-56 camera mounted in the aircraft's belly and fitted with a 3 inch lens, secures low-level panoramic (horizon to horizon) shots

Opposite below S/Sgt Marc Madero loads a 600 frame film cassette onto the back of a KA-56, while S/Sgt James Wheatley carries out some maintenance on the Radar Warning Receiver (RWR) antenna

Above The High Rollers have a C-12J for positioning crews, cargo and VIPs about the countryside

Front Office

Back Office

Above In the event of an inflight double generator failure, a ram-air-turbine (RAT) seen here, can be deployed pneumatically into the airstream. Its twin variable pitch turbine blades spool up to a constant 12,000 rpm, generating 3000 volt/amps of power for 15 minutes

Right Where did I put my car keys? With external doors 101, 102 and 111 removed, a nightmare of wiring and plumbing is revealed. The brick red trunking supplies hot, high velocity bleed air from the 17th stage of each engine compressor, and ducts it over the wing. This delays flow separation which reduces turbulence and drag, thereby lowering the stall speed and allowing the RF-4 to land at a lower velocity

Opposite above From nose to tail, external access doors 504, 6, 128, 33, 37 and 64 have been removed. In addition, the seldom used photoflash cartridge ejector doors (painted red and located in front of panel 64) are open

Opposite below Undergoing a 600-hour, periodic maintenance inspection, M/Sgt Duane Salisbury and S/Sgts Corey Beattie and Dan Tourville extract a J79-15 from the left engine bay of 832

Above Displaying its US Navy heritage, the aircraft in the background has its outer wing panels folded to the vertical position. They are locked in the spread position by nine lock pins. If the master pin is unlocked, a red warning light illuminates on the front cockpit telelight panel

Left M/Sgt Lubin Espinosa repositions stator blades in the compressor section of a J79 on completion of a 1400-hour engine inspection. At the 2400-hour stage depot maintenance is carried out at Tinker AFB, Oklahoma

Above In the Non-Destructive Inspection shop, engine oil mixed with Xylene is being analysed through an Atomic Absorption Spectrophotometer by T/Sgt Jeff Truitt. This can detect traces of chrome, iron, silver, aluminium, copper and magnesium, highlighting areas of wear and possible failure, which may require further trouble-shooting

Opposite above T/Sgt Ken Shoop checks out a new APQ-172 radar display unit. These will soon replace the APQ-99 sets, thereby considerably enhancing mission capability

Opposite below S/Sgt Eric Kolbe and A1 Class Doug Barron trouble-shoot an APQ-99 radar unit in the avionics shop. Note the old analog control unit

Above S/Sgts Jim Wallis and James Wheatley bench test the highly effective ALQ-101 Electronic Countermeasures (ECM) pod

NASA

In 1971 the NASA Airborne Science and Applications Program (ASAP) was set up to gather data from three principle areas, namely atmospheric data within the stratosphere, earth and celestial observations using electronic sensors and finally photographic. Two U-2Cs (56-6681, NASA serial 708 and 56-6682, NASA 709) were transferred directly from the CIA to NASA, providing a versatile, cost-effective, high altitude platform from where experiments could be conducted above 95 per cent of the Earth's atmosphere. At 70,000 feet, the aircraft is also above 97 per cent of the Earth's radiometric absorbers, so providing quality imagery, similar to that collected by sensors aboard satellites.

Today, the high altitude element of this invaluable programme utilizes an ER-2 (Earth Resources) and an ex-USAF TR-1 (Tactical Reconnaissance). The latter is due to be replaced at the time of writing by a second purpose-built ER-2, serial 80-1097. The ER-2 is almost identical to its military cousin, the TR-1. Indeed, the first ER-2 delivered to NASA, 80-1063, NASA serial 706, served effectively as the aerodynamic prototype for the TR-1 series. The TR-1, 80-1069, NASA 708, has taken aboard the same NASA serial of the now retired U-2C

Left The differing characteristics of the early U-2s and the TR-1 are obvious

Left While allocated to the 17th Reconnaissance Wing at RAF Alconbury, England, and parked on a hardstand on the night of 18 October 1983, a bus was inadvertantly driven into the then all black 80-1069. Receiving substantial damage the aircraft was repaired at Palmdale, California, and later loaned to NASA. As a result of the incident, the bus was written off and 069 is the only known U-2/TR-1 with a confirmed kill!

Above Operated by 'the Agency' as a U-2A, G and C, having been launched and recovered from the carrier deck of USS *Ranger*, and finally being involved in the HASP (High Altitude Airsampling Program), NASA 709 had already undertaken a varied career before being demobbed and put to work in civvy street

Left TR-1 Office. The telelight warning panel was illuminated for the benefit of the camera

Below In the cramped confines of a U-2C cockpit, Jim Hoyt undergoes a suit check in his S 100 partial pressure suit

Above Outboard wing sections folded, 708 is eased back into the hanger

Opposite above Located in the Q bay of 709 (and typical of the camera layout once carried by the agency and USAF), this A-3 configuration consists of three HR-732 cameras each with a 24 inch lens cone. This provides for multi-emulsion or multi-spectral coverage of the same ground area, which would measure 4 × 8 nm from 65,000 feet, giving a ground resolution of between two and 15 feet

Opposite below The U-2s, ER-2 and TR-1 of NASA have been the platforms of many varied experiments including the collection of 'cosmic dust', observations of severe thunderstorms, investigation into the transportation of pollutants into the stratosphere, measurement of fluorocarbon and hydrocarbon levels and their effect upon the ozone layer, observation of forest wildfires in California, the photo mapping of Alaska to a resolution of ten feet and many, many others

Dragons at Beale

Flying an aircraft solo in the corner of its flight envelope for protracted periods of time, while additionally gathering data of strategic importance, requires pilots of the highest calibre. Pilots flying the U-2 and TR-1 undertake such tasks daily. It is the job of the 5th Strategic Reconnaissance Training Sqn (SRTS), 9th Strategic Reconnaissance Wing (SRW) located at Beale AFB, California to train them.

Once checked out on type, these seasoned pilots are posted to one of two operational squadrons. Namely, either the 95th Reconnaissance Sqn (RS) 17th Reconnaissance Wing (RW) at RAF Alconbury, England, or the 99th SRS, 9th SRW.

The 9th SRW operates three U-2R detachments, manned by 99th SRS crews and aircraft: Detachment (Det) 2 at Osan AB, South Korea, Det 3 at RAF Akrotiri, Cyprus, and Det 5 at Patrick AFB, Florida (Det 1 and Det 4 are SR-71 detachments, operating from Kadena AB, Okinawa and RAF Mildenhall, England respectively). Det 6 at Norton AFB, California serves as a combined U-2/TR-1/SR-71 flight test centre where new avionics, electronic defence and sensor systems can be thoroughly evaluated before being deployed on the operational fleet.

With the student pilot in the
forward cockpit and his Instructor
Pilot (IP) aft, an early lesson is
learned concerning the wide turn
radius and the necessity of
anticipation while taxiing the U-2

Main picture Originally delivered in an overall white scheme, the first two-seat TR-1B trainer, 80-1064, holds short of the active runway

Inset Having received clearance from Air Traffic Control, 80-1065, the second TR-1B to be delivered, lines up on the runway. Brakes are applied and an engine check ensures normal operation prior to take-off

Right Take-off clearance received, brakes are released and the TR-1's J75 engine is spooled up to take-off power. The pilot concentrates on keeping the long, high aspect ratio wings level

Above As the wings get airborne the pogo wheels drop away

Far Right Airborne in just over 1000 feet of runway, a U-2R/TR-1 reaches 50,000 feet in about 15–20 minutes. The earlier, lighter C models could reach the same altitude in about 10 minutes

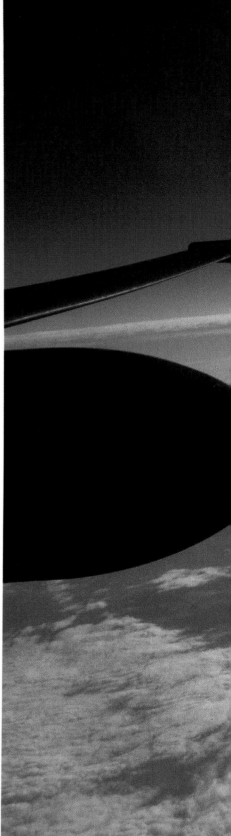

Above Nearing the corner of the flight envelope it becomes difficult to determine the difference between Mach buffet and stall buffet. Both are to be avoided and the margin between the two can be just 5 knots. An autopilot has to be used if flight in this region is to be sustained. (Photo courtesy of Major John Bowen)

Inset Through a system of prisms and mirrors, the Baird Scientific drift sight provides the pilot with complete optical coverage of the world below his aircraft and is used for pinpoint navigation. (Photo courtesy of Major John Bowen)

Main picture At 70,000 feet, line-of-sight distance is about 320 nm, but what can you distinguish at that range? 'Well, depending on sun-angle and the prevailing weather, it's possible to see a coastline. A city could be seen only at night, by its lights. A mountain range would probably be indicated by the cu (cumulous clouds) built up over it. The curvature of the Earth isn't too well defined because the water molecules in the troposphere often create a layer of haze. However, as the Sun goes up or down through the terminator (the line dividing the illuminated and dark part of the planet), it is possible to see the curvature of the Earth.'—U-2 pilot. (Courtesy of Major John Bowen)

Above The 5th SRTS (Strategic Reconnaissaince Training Sqn) uses the call sign PINION followed by a two-figure crew number

Right 'Descent out of the corner of the flight envelope is by default. If you lower the nose, you speed up, enter Mach buffet and shortly after enter Mach tuck—that's where the tail of the airplane flips over its nose. If you ease back on the power you stall. If you try to initiate recovery by pushing the nose down you'll enter Mach tuck again. So you have to deploy the speed brakes and drop the gear. In this way you increase drag, lose between 500–1000 feet of altitude, and the 'window' opens a couple of knots. Now you can ease off some power and lose a bit more height. This 'milking' process continues down to 60,000 feet and can take 10 minutes!—U-2 pilot

Above In the pattern, the U-2 pilot's main concern is fuel-balancing the wing tanks ready for landing. As there is only a fuel totalizer gauge, fuel has to be transferred from one wing tank to the other until the control yoke is trimmed level. The pogos remain in place during the early stages of conversion on type in order to minimize possible wingtip damage on landing

Right With full flap and a 10 knot headwind, the pilot aims for a point 10 feet up and about 200 feet in the overrun. On reaching this point the throttle is closed to idle and the aircraft driven down one to two feet, where it is held until it stalls

Main picture If wind conditions allow and the fuel is correctly balanced, the U-2 will sit on its centre gear while a team from maintenance secures the pogos

Above Should it all go pear-shaped, punishment for the student can be harsh!

Inset Having bought three TR-1Bs, the U-2CTs were retired. This particular U-2 (56-6953) was the second such aircraft to have been built from the surviving parts of damaged U-2s. It is seen here at Beale AFB in November 1986. Note the drag chute

Above On 2 August 1988, General Rogers, Commander-in-Chief of Strategic Air Command (in pressure suit on left) experienced at first hand a high altitude familiarization flight in a TR-1B

Main picture TR-1B, 80-1091 basks on the ramp under the California sun

Inset Snoopy gives Woodstock some flying lessons on the tail of this TR-1B. Tail art is supplied in chalk only—presumably for ease of removal in the event of official objections

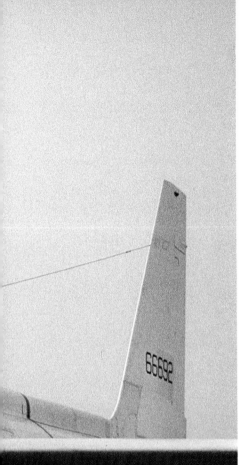

56-6692 was the first U-2CT to be built at Lockheed's Palmdale plant. Pictured at RAF Alconbury in October 1988, this historic aircraft is slowly being destroyed while undergoing damage control maintenance—note repair panel below front windscreen

The traffic pattern at Beale is a
constant source of activity

The main undercarriage
arrangement of the U-2/TR-1 is
unique

The vast size of Beale AFB—23,000 acres—together with its remote
location, enables training to continue unabated well into the evening

Left TR-1, 80-1076 comes to a halt and drops one wing

Above Properly secured, the pogos will align themselves as the aircraft begins to taxi

Left TR-1, 80-1082, a particularly well worn example, awaits take-off clearance

Above Equipped with short nose but super-pods, 082 nears rotate speed

Opposite TR-1, 80-1087 gets back from a high altitude check flight

Above U-2R, 69-10338 has a high altitude air sampling unit bolted into its Q bay

Left Tail art, U-2R style

Far left All U-2s and TR-1s are equipped with an externally mounted rear-view mirror

Above Mission over, the pilot has already disconnected the helmet from the rest of the pressure suit

Left Probably the most exotic operational reconnaissance aircraft ever built, the Lockhhed SR-71, is co-billeted with its Lockheed forerunner at Beale

Above Alone and unarmed

Brake chute cover in the descent
and main chute about to blossom,
64-17956, the sole surviving
SR-71B two-seat trainer, touches
down and taxies in

Toujours au Danger

The 17th Reconnaissance Wing, motto *Toujours au Danger*—'Ever in Danger', and its flying component, the 95th Reconnaissance Sqn, were activated at RAF Alconbury on 1 October 1982 and became operational five months later. SAC is responsible for providing administrative, logistical and training support, whilst day to day tasking is conducted by USAFE. A list of reconnaissance collection areas is submitted by various NATO agencies; these are prioritized and incorporated into a mission plan. When communicated to the 17th RW, mission planners feed a collection plan and navigation track into MOBFPS (Main Operating Base Flight Planning System). This computer correlates all details to produce a route to fly and a digitized chip which, when installed on the aircraft, will automatically activate the relevant sensor systems.

The unit operates the TR-1 which, except for some internal wiring, is identical to the U-2R. It is the operational role which 'separates' the two types; with the U-2R supporting the US strategic data base and the TR-1 being a NATO asset which, although owned and operated by SAC, would report directly to the Supreme Allied Commander in Europe in times of crisis or in a war situation.

Left Doors rolled back and early morning fog filling hangar 4004, TR-1 80-1086 awaits the start of another day's flying

Right Wearing an S 1010B full pressure suit and helmet, Major Steve Nichols boards 80-1088 for a high altitude operational sortie to Germany. There is no truth in the rumour that the 17th RW's rear motto is 'Two Jerks In Danger'

Lined up, these two shots illustrate the difference between the super-pods and nose sections that are fitted to this airframe while on operations and when training

Above Steve Nichols taxies KONA 17 out to the holding point. Note the extensive antenna farm under the fuselage and right super-pod, used to 'hoover up' a wide range of Electronic Intelligence (ELINT). This aircraft is also equipped with the Northrop NAS-21A Astro Inertial Navigation System. Most of the other aircraft flown by the 95th RS are equipped with the less expensive Litton LN-33 INS

Above TR-1s bound for Germany usually reach 60,000 feet about 30 miles south of Amsterdam, where upon they turn off their mode 'Charlie' height read-out, which makes it more difficult to ascertain their operational altitude

Covered in blisters and bumps, the nose houses a Mechanically Steered or Electrically Steered Antenna (MSA/ESA). This dual planar array antenna is part of the high resolution, Advanced Synthetic Aperture Radar System (ASARS-2) produced for the TR-1 by Hughes. It transmits its digitized information via a data link (located in the radome under the tail) to a ground unit, where the information is displayed in near real-time. (Courtesy Major John Bowen)

Both short and empty ASARS configured nose sections are flown during circuit training to enable pilots to remain familiar with the different out-of-cockpit perspectives and characteristics offered by each. Here, 80-1093, call sign ROOK 23, flown by Captain Dom Eanniello, prepares for another touch and go

Above Driving either a 5-litre Ford Mustang or an El Camino, a qualified U-2 pilot drives behind a landing U-2 and counts down the height to go before touchdown. This enables the pilot to keep his eyes out of the cockpit and those long wings nice and level

Right Here Mobile Control in an El Camino oversees a touch-and-go flown by Major John Bowen in 80-1086, call sign ROOK 20

Low sun and camera angle combine to give Major Blaine Bachus flying 093, call sign ROOK 32, a deceptively high take-off angle

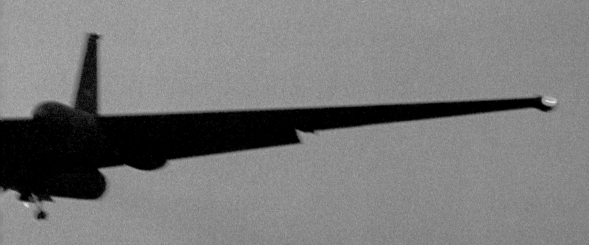

The 95th RS uses the call sign ROOK for its training sorties. This is followed by the pilot's two-figure crew number. Here ROOK 32 flies another go-around

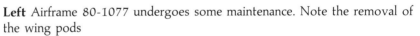

Left Airframe 80-1077 undergoes some maintenance. Note the removal of the wing pods

Preceding pages A mission bird in the hangar sports yet another combination of super-pods and nose section

Above A close up of the tip skid and RHAW gear; the latter is said to offer outstanding hemispherical coverage

Overleaf The outer wing sections of the U-2R/TR-1 fold, enabling the aircraft to use a standard US Navy aircraft carrier elevator, should such a deployment become necessary